MAGDALENA BAK·MAIER

MAKE TIME COUNT

FOR THOSE WHO WISH FOR A BETTER LIFE

SO THEY CAN MAKE IT HAPPEN.

"Man surprised me most about humanity. Because he sacrifices his health in order to make money. Then he sacrifices money to recuperate his health. And then he is so anxious about the future that he does not enjoy the present; the result being that he does not live in the present or the future; he lives as if he is never going to die, and then dies having never really lived."

- Dalai Lama -

THE GET PRODUCTIVE GRID: A SIMPLE AND PROVEN
WORK/LIFE BALANCE SYSTEM TO HELP YOU THRIVE.

C O N T E N T S

- MAKING YOUR OWN YEAR GRID –

- ADVANCING BALANCE AND ACTION WITH THE MONTH GRID -

- 3 MONTH REVIEW -

- BECOMING A MASTER OF PRACTICE -

What you seek, is seeking you.

- Rumi

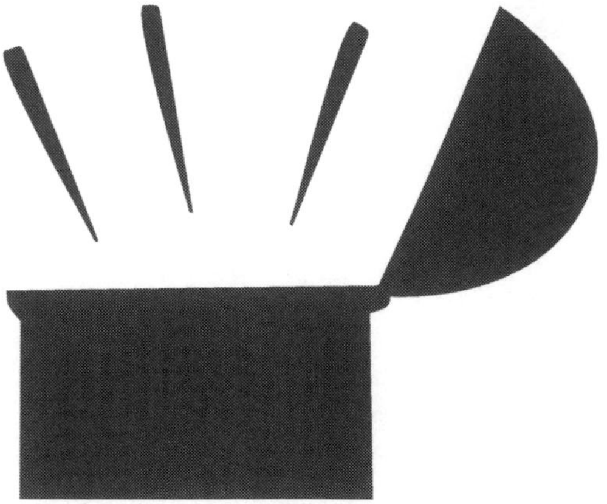

PREFACE

This book is a manual that aims to introduce you to the Grid, why it's needed, how it works, and to assist you in building and experimenting with your own Grids. Grid is an original tool I have created which I really believe helps people create better, healthier, more productive lives.

I have kept the content practical and directly relevant as if you were in one of my in-person workshops. But of course the Grid is a tool and so you will need time to put it to use and assess how it is working for you. This book will support you in this process. For those who want to know the science behind the Grid, look at my blogs on LinkedIn or www.maketimecount.com. My aim here is to get you to jump straight in and experiment! I want you to start creating your wonderful life right now!

I have been experimenting with the Grid design for many years. I'm no stranger to a fast paced life, massive changes, upheavals and setbacks, as well as a drive and desire to improve my conditions. Like you, I want a good life and I'm happy to work hard at it. First, I deeply believe we all deserve one but results happen when we take responsibility and do the work. Second, I can think of people who as far as I can tell have such a life already. Third, I am committed to the idea of working towards making my life be fantastic, rather than settling for one that isn't.

The Grid came out of my own need for balance as a tool to help me keep my resolve and attend to things that would somehow always slip from my busy agenda. For me this was

health and focus on spending time not working. I wanted time for friends and family, trying a new class, finding time for exercise, doing something wacky and new, or even idling time away on occasion. I also wanted to make time for writing books and building my coaching practice. And I wanted time for rest and holidays.

The Gridding practice helps me create and uphold better habits, keeps me focused on what I want to do instead of what I feel drifts in, and supports me in creating the life that makes me happy. Before I knew it, I was helping my clients design their lives using Grids for support and then being a trained scientists holding small study groups to systematically assess what made the Grid work for others, in some cases over a number of years. What I saw was amazing and truly encouraging. We could start with people completely out of balance or missing a sense of direction and hope, those overrun by life or those complaining of never having 'enough time' and help them change their lives for the better.

You see I am convinced that lives can be fulfilling, healthy, rich with joy, genuine connection and success. That each of us has the capacity and means to create the sort of life we can't wait to get up for. I believe we can have it all provided we know how to define what "all" means and that we learn to stay on top of it. The Grid is a tool that helps me do that and I believe will help you also.

INTRODUCTION

ABOUT MAGDALENA BAK - MAIER

Magdalena Bak-Maier helps people connect heart and mind and live it. Magdalena is a talent developer, educator, researcher, author and the founder of Make Time Count, a company and eco-system devoted to empowering individuals and organisations to succeed and thrive. Her incisive models and tools have enabled a variety of teams (among them senior NASA engineers, CEOs and NHS Doctors) to challenge conventional thinking, tackle turbulence and complexity and deliver outstanding results, while learning how to nurture themselves and others. Her Get Productive Grid is a simple and proven holistic system to help people balance life and work and to excel. Grid is Magdalena's contribution to help transform the wellbeing agenda from government policy into personal practice. In the Grid, Madgalena merges her extensive science training (PhD, Caltech) with many years of helping people get more out of their lives. She lives in London.

A HEARTFELT WELCOME FROM THE AUTHOR

It's an honour for me to be able to guide you as you explore ways to make time count for you. Helping people to follow their heart and make use of their full brainpower is my vocation. Everyone has talent. The question is how to pin it down and develop it to serve the individual and the world. I have developed the Grid system as a powerful holistic productivity tool, to help you identify your personal and professional goals, and to give you a framework in which to attend to them all so that you can live your life in a way which is authentic, decisive and inspiring. The Grid will help you look after your career and yourself so that you can be and give the best of yourself through regular renewal so that you can thrive in balance.

I'm often struck by how tantalisingly close many of us are to a life of joy, yet struggle along settling for less, burning out in jobs that don't fulfil us and neglecting our wellbeing until we become cynical and jaded by life. The media keeps selling us a world where that joyful feeling of "having it all" seems attainable, yet is always frustratingly just out of reach. In my many years of coaching teams and individuals across all walks of life, one thing has become clear: our biggest barriers to joy are not the external factors imposed upon us, but the obstacles we put in our own way. My research shows that barriers typically include: being unclear about what we want, not having systems to organise our lives and not having the confidence to put our plans into action. Common to all of these is an imbalance between what our head says and what our heart desires.

So how do we deal with these barriers? Generally, we avoid them; we take the path of least resistance. This may seem like a good idea for a while, but long-term it makes us feel regretful, unfulfilled and conflicted. We are left with the nagging feeling that deep down we desire something else – or simply something more, that we are wasting our lives and, in effect, keeping ourselves shackled through our own choices and habits.

So why do we settle for less? In my experience, as much as we long for change, we often fear it; specifically, we fear disappointment. It's much easier to stick with what we know, what's predictable or routine, even if the result is that we feel overwhelmed, unfulfilled or simply stuck.

But the good news is that this fear is almost always unfounded. I have helped hundreds of clients navigate change with the Grid system – and no one who has applied it has been disappointed yet! As a neuroscientist and coach, I know how to work with the brain to support our dreams, so that we feel comfortable with change. And, by the way, the whole "I need to change" mantra is somewhat of a misguided concept. A more accurate phrase in all circumstances would be "live more fully in our true potential".

As we go along, I'll share with you why using the Grid will support you in creating a life you love, right from the first week you get started. People working with The Grid love how they feel and the results they create. Feelings of conflict between 'have tos' and 'want tos', between head and heart fall away. The Grid helps you stay focused and be holistically productive. It realigns your desire with your know how for greater balance, results that matter and connects you with life and other people. Because the Grid looks after all aspects of your life, it naturally refuels you – giving you energy and time you didn't know you had.

19

WHO IS THE GRID FOR?

The Grid is for you if you find yourself saying...

- 'I work hard but feel I'm not getting anywhere.'
- 'I lack time for life outside my work (dating, hobbies, friends, holidays or family).'
- 'My to-do list is never-ending.'
- 'I don't have energy for anything other than work and need weekends to recover.'
- 'I'm settling for less because "having it all" seems unattainable.'

Once you start applying the Grid approach to your life, you will start to feel clear, inspired and energised. The Grid will help you balance your energy and effort in a way that restores you and helps you achieve more. Committed 'Gridders' find that they live more in tune with their values, that they begin to move towards the life they truly want. In fact, what happens is that their heart and mind get on the same track and they no longer procrastinate.

HOW TO USE THIS BOOK

This is a practical book you can easily read from cover to cover in one or two sittings. Doing this will give you a good overview of what the Grid is and how it works. I suggest that you read the book twice. You may wish to start creating your own Year Grid and Monthly Grid after the first reading, but I'm sure there will be small details you may miss that will fall into place on rereading the book. Use your Grids and give it about three to four months before you review how the practice has helped you.

For regular updates, like-minded community, and blogs related to Gridding please check out www.maketimecount.com

23

MAGDALENA BAK - MAIER

WHY DO WE NEED NEW TOOLS TO HELP US BE PRODUCTIVE?

Our lives have become increasingly busy and complex. In today's world it is easier than ever to be occupied but not necessarily to be productive because at the heart of productivity sits one's ability to dare to imagine, dream and envisage a life that for too many people seems impossible. Many people I have and will work with will say something like:

"It's not possible to have an amazing partner, in the end they always disappoint."

"I can't afford the life I want to have and don't see how I ever will be able to."

"What's the point of trying to be good when everyone around me is such a s***?"

"Why risk failure or rejection when I can just do what I'm doing now?"

"Who will actually love the real me? "

"I will never become big, talented, top etc"

The same people will often

- Take their partners for granted, let them down and self-sabotage the relationship.
- Pretend they don't care about money and wealth.
- Get frustrated and angry that the world is not overrun with people that are just like them.
- Stay put instead of working towards their true aspirations or even taking steps to find out what they may be.
- Focus on pleasing others at their own expense, sacrifice and suffering.
- Bury their talents and skills but watch others with admiration.

To all those people I want to say:

Stop!
Listen!
Learn that alternatives are possible!

Life is made of choices and much of what we get is a function of what we are willing to do to make things happen. By this I mean working hard and smart. Working in balance with our very being and the world in which we live. This means we have to be awake.

Life can be beautiful, exciting and even lucky when you decide to show up and take responsibility. In other words, when you are willing to work for it.

Many people say they are but in reality few really do! This is why we all need a coach in some area of our life. Good coaches help fuel hearts and make us think. Their support is vital as are tools such as the Grid that we can use oursleves. Those who have the will, desire, hunger, passion and sense of ambition need tools, frameworks and models to make their dreams and ideas happen. For those who lack ambition and drive such tools are a must!

This is true for a number of reasons. Below, are my Top three:

• We all like to see evidence to sustain our belief in something. Not having the right tools means results take longer to realize. Without seeing progress, many people give up too soon when the productive thing would be to keep going.
• Much of success in life is linked with being able to sustain productivity over the long haul and this is virtually impossible without support structures, tools and learning how to do this on purpose as opposed to by accident. Being productive also requires regular audits so that we are not reacting to life or being blinkered. Productive people create lives that help them become better people. In other words our action supports our evolution.
• Self-awareness is the bedrock of creating a fulfilling life. Without it people can create lives they later want to leave instead of enjoying. This is, in my view, the biggest waste of time and talent. Hence I believe one of the key priorities for those who claim to be productive is personal development.

This book is designed to equip you with a useful framework and tool to be holistically productive, to feel in charge of your life, and in creating conditions that inspire and refuel you.

WHAT EXACTLY IS THE GET PRODUCTIVE GRID?

The Grid is a way of identifying your personal and professional goals and helping you achieve them by setting them out in a clear and accessible four-part Grid format. What's more, it's a life plan that looks after your mind and your heart. It's entirely personal to you and remains flexible. As you grow and your priorities change, the Grid evolves with you.

First, I'll show you how to draw up a 'Year Grid', which sets out everything you want to accomplish in the next 12 months. Then, we'll make a Grid for the coming month, where we look at more immediate goals. Once you master the Grid way of thinking, working and living, you can use this approach over whatever time frame suits you best.

A year is a good time frame to start with. It is a substantial amount of time in which one can achieve a great deal and change the quality of your life completely. Having a yearly Grid makes it then easier to create shorter Grids (monthly, weekly, daily) that support the larger year blueprint.

IS THE GRID JUST A FANCY TO-DO LIST?

Many people when they first learn my Grid method ask whether the Grid is just another way to make a To-do list. The answer is No! The Grid is far more than a To-do list. The Grid is a superior way of keeping track of and staying on top of what we want to do. Here's why.

To-do lists keep us in reactive mode

To-do lists are often skewed towards work and life commitments that are urgent and non-negotiable and may miss out equally meaningful but less tangible aspects of life. For many people To-do lists capture what they know they need to do. As such many To-do lists are highly reactive. Such lists keep people stuck in life patterns rather than helping them create lives that are more balanced and well rounded. In other words To-do lists by themselves do not help people master life. Finally, most To-do lists are often not that well aligned with the reality of what's happening in our life nor in terms of what we want out of life. Those who have a big To-do list have in effect a memory aid of things they need and want to do, while in reality they often cope with whatever comes. If that sounds like you, then it means you are spending most of your time working on what's urgent instead of working on what's important. Hence To-do lists keep us reacting to life where the right tool should be aiding us in being proactive artists of the life we want to have.

To-do lists lack effective structure to help our minds work at their best

Our brains can't help but make lists. It is what they do. When we commit these ideas to paper we free up the mind from having to constantly work to remember it. However, a typical To-do list lacks sufficient structure to be useful. The mind likes to cluster things into categories so that it can juggle information efficiently, and be most resourceful. Without tasks being categorized, or you having multiple To-do lists, trying to stay on top of things via a To-do list is difficult. The more you have to do the more it can feel like all you're doing is "chasing your tail". The order of

27

items in a To-do list has little or no relation to their relative importance for your life. It is often simply the way your mind recalled what needed doing. Without project management software or at least fields for deadlines and other ways to create some sense of priority, a To-do list muddles the most capable mind.

To-do lists often impede productivity by sapping energy

The longer the To-do list becomes, the more daunting it looks and feels. To-do lists force our attention to the top items because our minds are used to looking for what's at the 'top of the list', 'needs to get done' or 'what's got an imminent deadline?'. As many To-do lists lack true currency, often the most productive task is not at the top at all. It may not even be on the list. In such cases, the To-do list becomes a barrier to action instead of an aid. By the time you scan it you begin to feel burdened by the sheer amount of what looks like work, and lose energy and motivation to tackle it. Rewriting To-do lists over and over can help lists be current, but this activity takes time away from doing actual work.

To-do lists are rarely motivating because they are poorly executed

Most items on a To-do list are rarely expressed as single tasks to be done. While this is more to do with having a good technique for writing To-do lists in the first place, most To-do lists suffer from poor task definition. Many items on a To-do list are in reality goals. And goals are often projects that require a series of steps to get done. This means that trying to get through a To-do list of goals can leave you demotivated, overwhelmed, and in an unproductive state. This happens because while it feels like you have worked hard and long, your list does not diminish much or at all.

To-do lists often are not physically positioned to be a useful memory and focus aid

The mind drifts naturally and is easily distracted so tools that help remind us what we should be doing aid our productivity. However, too many To-do lists end up locked away on a computer or other electronic device as files, live on pages of yet another journal or notebook, or are put away somewhere instead of being readily visible. In this way a To-do list fails to achieve one of its key jobs – helping you stay focused, take responsibility for what happens in your life, and how you use your time. Calendars and diaries can supplement this, but they can be too prescriptive by telling us what we need to do at a specific time, when a far more productive way to use time would be to do something else instead.

To-do lists are rarely comprehensive and so they can drive us into greater imbalance

To-do lists are often devoted to one area instead of one's complete life. Many people for example have a work To-do list but not a To-do life list. To-do lists are rarely truly comprehensive and well considered. To truly take advantage of lists you would need to make one for each life area that matters to you. This is the principle behind the concept of the Life Wheel many coaches use. But Life Wheels are often focused on determining factual starting points so that the impact of coaching can be evaluated. What one then needs to stay productive are other tools to keep on track.

To-do lists are boring (for some people)

Finally, for more creative people, To-do lists are simply boring. So while in principle and with good technique To-do lists can aid us in getting things done, many people simply won't do them and so they need an alternative.

HOW THE GRID HELPS IN A WAY TO-DO LISTS CAN'T

The Grid is creative! It uses colour. The Grid also provides a broad conceptual framework but its implementation remains highly personalized. This means that the Grid can suit people with different lifestyles, personal preferences and personalities. Gridding can actually be fun!

Grids are designed to be comprehensive. They support people's lives in total, including their wellbeing. The Grid is designed to capture all your key priorities on a single sheet of paper. And it ensures that what you capture is current! In other words what's on your Grid (and hence your agenda) has relevance for you in the present and takes you towards the future you desire.

The Grid is something you consult and interact with on a daily basis. It is your map and compass where you can relate the big picture for your life (Year Grid) with specific goals and steps that will take you there (Month Grid). This means you are always reminded about what's important and what needs to happen whilst you are also free to choose how it happens. The Grid also helps you keep track of your progress with colour by getting you to highlight what has been achieved. This means that every time you look at the Grid, your mind has a powerful visual cue that reminds you of how productive you already are!

By outlining the work to be done or action to be taken as true tasks (activities that can be achieved in one go), the Grid focuses the mind on specific work steps that build towards the larger goals. This fuels your motivation and gives you energy to make quicker progress. The Grid is highly motivating in terms of productivity because you are constantly working to help yourself refuel – it's what the Grid design emphasizes. And, the Grid helps you feel good because all actions on it are truly task-based. This means you will complete them faster and derive a sense of progress and satisfaction. Most Gridders get more done in a day than people without a Grid.

The Grid is designed to help you surf your energy levels and match it to tasks. By capturing everything in one place – the Grid page – the Grid gives you total control and responsibility for making best use of your energy and time against it. So the Grid supports people working in a real context as opposed to one their mind imagines.

The Grid forces you to be proactive because in order to create your Grid (be it for the year or the upcoming month), you have to first imagine the life you want. This means that the Grid helps to *coach* you. Regular Grid use helps you develop your own practice of being and staying productive. Past Grids are like diaries where you can spot what got done, what didn't, and what your life actually looks like.

FOLLOWING THE GRID HELPS ME:

- Stay on top of my health.
- Attend to and work with what's important most of the time instead of reacting to what's coming in.
- Show up and create a rich personal life.
- Develop my business and career.
- Feel less overwhelmed and more in control of what in effect is a very full agenda.
- Build my confidence and sense of mastery.
- Enjoy a guilt-free sense of free time to be spontaneous and creative.

would not think of all this with a To-do list.

As a neuroscientist I can see why. The Grid more closely matches how the mind works. It helps the user with clarity, focus, priorities, goal setting, creation of plans, taking responsibility, managing energy, and developing a vision for what they want life to look and feel like.

Once mastered, the Grid supports people in creating great lives whilst being and feeling more complete as a person.

In my experience effective people divide into two broad types: those with goals and those who don't see the point of them. Where the first group moves from point to point via clearly marked stepping stones, the second group explores and moves forward towards whatever in their judgment shows best promise or seems most satisfactory. Each is a valid way of being in life and each can be extremely successful and fulfilling. What both groups share is a goal to pursue happiness.

So whether you want to set specific goals that together seem to create your life masterpiece such as a new house, more satisfying job, fulfilling relationships, or a feeling you make a difference, or simply need to explore different options available to you at this moment in time, being clearer about what you want your life to be like and feel like, will help you live more on purpose.

My invitation to you is to become more conscious of your life and more mindful of how you create it.

34

HOLISTIC
PRODUCTIVITY

WHY DO WE NEED WORK-LIFE BALANCE?

Work-life balance is an important marker in terms of people's wellbeing and family life. Time devoted to leisure, self-care, social and other non-work based activities helps individuals remain healthy and productive over time. Obtaining the best possible lifestyle balance for each individual is a concern for each of us, for those we live with, work and love, as well as for employers and governments in terms of business and policy decisions because it relates to our general wellbeing. It's not just about working long hours and having time for leisure activities. Our wellbeing is also linked with social connections, life satisfaction and our environment.

Below are a few statistics on work-life balance and wellbeing that highlight the need for and relevance of work-life balance, and tools such as the Grid.

- In 2014 work-life balance comes second only to salary as the key factor that makes an employer attractive for over 65% of respondents across 230,000 workers across different industries and age groups in 31 countries (Kelly Services © Statista 2015).

- 1 in 10 workers would like to work 11.2 fewer hours than they currently do for less pay according to the Office of National Statistics UK 2014 report on underemployment and overemployment. (Annual Population Survey Dataset).

- Over 1 million hard-working small business owners compromise family and social life due to work pressures according to Simply Business - the UK's biggest business insurance provider 2014 survey of over 300,000 small business customers.

- The cost of sickness and unemployment in the UK alone is estimated at £100 billion a year. according to a 2014 Department of Work and Pensions report.

Work-life balance
matters more than we REALISE.

MAGDALENA BAK - MAIER

WORK-LIFE BALANCE IS A STATE OF MIND

We all know that work-life balance is important for health, happiness and the ability to work effectively. Companies and legislation have made great strides in flexible working practices, because they know it creates a happier, more productive and loyal workforce. And yet I still come across countless individuals who have all the flexible working policies at their disposal, but say that they are overworked with no time for the things and people that matter to them.

True work-life balance is so much more than flexible working. It's a state of mind. It's about you as an individual. This is my unique focus - and where my specially-devised Grid comes into its own.

A well-balanced life - where you are clear about all the things that matter to you and have time to give to them - represents a healthier and more sustainable approach to living and working. Most importantly, it's more fulfilling. It means not having to make sacrifices or suffer the painful inner conflict that inevitably arises when we make work/life trade-offs.

Imagine how good it would feel to know that you are living a balanced life and shaping your future in a way that reflects your values, your interests and your personality. The Grid can help you do all this. It means you never put yourself at the bottom of your to-do list. Many people are doing this successfully already. Here's what these 'Gridders' said:

"Remarkably, I had more time during the last few weeks, which has felt a lot better. It gave me massive clarity of focus and a huge sense of success, as I have managed to tick pretty much everything off....I love the power of attraction and it is true; you do get in life what you focus on! "

"I would never be able to clear this amount of work before and yet I am finding time for more still and my family life has improved a lot according to my wife :)"

"It's taken a while to feel like I no longer chase my tail but now three months in, I would never give this system up. "

*"Absolute life saver! This is 'the secret!' only you're sharing it.
Thank you."*

40

THE GET PRODUCTIVE GRID

HOLISTIC PRODUCTIVITY

You're interested in living more, working well, and doing things better, which is why you have turned to the Get Productive Grid. 'Productivity' is all about getting things done; but we're not machines. It's not just our output that matters, but the impact it has on us and on those around us. In other words, what matters is our wellbeing and the results we create.

I like to think in terms of 'holistic productivity' which is how I'm determined to redefine what productivity means. Holistic productivity is all about achieving results and your goals but it's also about looking after yourself in order to keep your energy in a cycle of constant renewal and your mind and body in good condition. This includes being mindful of how you impact others.
As the lines between work and life become increasingly blurred, the Grid becomes an indispensible tool to help you look after yourself.

For my top holistic productivity tips, see page 123.

DEVELOPING
CLARITY

HOW DO I IDENTIFY MY GOALS?

This is not always such an easy question to answer. Naming exactly what we want and need, can be a challenge. Before we tackle the Grid, we will complete three exercises to help you gather information about yourself: what's important to you in living a balanced and authentic life of joy at home and at work? What's holding you back? These exercises will help you identify the things you desire and want to realise as well as the balance you need to underpin this so that you are able to thrive.

GOAL
EXERCISES

THE GET PRODUCTIVE GRID

45

MAGDALENA BAK - MAIER

EXERCISE 1: EXPLORING THE IDEA OF THRIVING

Thriving is very different from surviving. Many people survive in life; very few truly thrive.

THRIVING IS A SET OF CONDITIONS SUPPORTING PROSPEROUS GROWTH

Becoming curious about the specific conditions, which help you thrive starts to bring your goals into focus – not just your work goals but those that improve your wellbeing.

Set aside 10-15 minutes for the following exercise.

- Imagine you are a beautiful, vibrant seed that will grow into a magnificent plant. You are destined to become the healthiest and best example of your species.

- Now imagine your seed breaking through tough, frozen soil - or maybe even concrete - in order to manifest its presence in the world.

- Picture your seed growing in truly difficult conditions, which involve a real struggle.

- You have survived but it took determination and a great deal of effort.

- Now see yourself on the same growth journey, only this time as a person. Put yourself in specific conditions to help you thrive, rather than those in which you struggle or simply survive.

- Become intensely curious about your personal 'microclimate' for optimum growth. See it in your mind's eye. Gather all the details about the specific place in which you find yourself.

- Ask yourself: who or what surrounds you in this specific place of growth? What do things look and sound like? What colours, smells, textures do you notice?

- What are you wearing in this place? Doing? Saying?

It's time to close your eyes and take yourself on a tour of your 'thriving space'. Let your mind's eye peek into every corner of what you see and hear. Explore as detailed a picture as possible.

When you have finished, trust that you will remember what you saw and experienced. You may wish to close your eyes while you do this exercise and dictate your vision to a phone recorder. Use the space below for notes.

Look back over your description. What are the key characteristics and values that come through? Some people notice that they value being with people or enjoy a sense of buzz, while others are drawn towards solitude and calm.

Note down a clear checklist of the conditions you need to thrive. You may have some already in place in your life. Others you may be able to create easily.
Write down how you would achieve them too.

EXERCISE 2: RECONNECTING THROUGH GENEROSITY

GENEROSITY IS A MINDSET TOOTED IN THE BELLIEF THAT WE HAVE ENOUGH

When we feel we have plenty, we are more likley to want to share. But how many of us truly believe we have enough? Most people, in fact, think the opposite. Generosity is the opposite of scarcity where we think that we, or those around us, don't have enough.

Practising generosity as a mindset is key to personal development. This is because generosity embeds our faith in things being better. It acknowledges the many ways in which our life already reflects abundance. We are then better able to tap into our blessings. Not only that, but we can start to convert those blessings into prosperity.

MAGDALENA BAK - MAIER

Think about your everyday environment. You can start at the micro level with the people you live with - family, friends, room mates, neighbours. Equally, you can start at the macro level, thinking about your occupation, gender, nationality, professional affiliations.

Now cast your mind back over the past few days or weeks to moments when you felt someone needed help. Pay close attention to situations in which you could have made a difference to them - helped them thrive, get ahead or overcome difficulty.

Now, note down three to five people, who you know could use your help right now. What sort of help could you offer? Note: don't think of going out of your way necessarily. Instead, think about activities you could do with little time and effort, that would make a big difference to this person.

Here are a few examples:
• offer to pick up groceries for my neighbour while doing my shopping
• introduce one person's work to another to open up an opportunity for them
• invite someone out
• share your newspapers or magazines with someone who appreciates them
• alert someone to an opportunity which they could benefit from.

51

MAGDALENA BAK - MAIER

Let's begin by looking at who you can help using the table below.

PEOPLE I CAN HELP

	WHO	WHAT	HOW
1.			
2.			
3.			
4.			
5.			

What's really interesting when we examine generosity in this way, is how often we pass up opportunites to practise generosity on a daily basis; yet we still expect the world to be generous towards us.

Once we practice giving and sharing our riches - be that via a smile, idea or resource - it puts us in a position to ask for help from others. In doing this, we give those we ask for help a gift of acknowledgement. We help them see their strengths, skills, abilities and wealth. We give them opportunities to practice generosity.

I am amazed how seldom many of my clients practice asking for help. So below, I invite you to note down three to five specific areas where you need help. Think about who could help you and how.

HELP I NEED RIGHT NOW

	WHAT I NEED?	WHO CAN HELP?	HOW?
1.			
2.			
3.			
4.			
5.			

Your task now is to practice generosity on a regular basis by sharing your gifts and inviting others to help you where you need help most. If you need a reminder, then incorporate generosity into your Grid, both in giving and in asking for the help you need.

EXERCISE 3: HEART AND MIND ALIGNMENT

'Heart and mind fusion' is the basis of all my work. It's how I help myself and the people I coach, to live a balanced and fulfilling life.

So what do I mean by 'heart and mind fusion'? Many people follow their heart but struggle to thrive. Others apply their capable minds to tackling problems that lack real meaning for them. Most people recognise that we need both heart and mind to thrive. Yet very few know how to integrate them.

Earlier, I mentioned that using the Grid could help you resolve inner conflict. This works because 'heart and mind fusion' is at the core of being and feeling in balance.

Heart and mind fusion
resolves inner conflict by
balancing our emotional and rational needs.

I strongly believe that heart and mind fusion work can also create positive change in our wider world (for a short animation watch my YouTube video 'Why Heart and Mind Fusion.' https://goo.gl/6XxLIL

MAGDALENA BAK - MAIER

The following exercise is one I use in many of my programmes, one-to-one work and in my own life to make sure I am living a life that satisfies every part of me.

Complete each of the 13 statements below. The goal here is not to provide an answer to every statement but rather to identify those that come *readily* to you. If an answer does not spring to mind, skip to the next statement and leave a blank.

In the past 12 months I....

1. took responsibility for...
2. binned...
3. began...

4. felt truly energized by...
5. called on others to...
6. made an impact in the following area/field/community etc...

7. faced...
8. honoured...
9. achieved...

10. made a priority...
11. made a plan for...
12. completed...

13. was deeply touched by the following things/people/events/ideas...

Now do the same again, but looking at the coming 12 months.

This year I really want to ...

1. take responsibility for...

2. bin...

3. begin...

4. feel truly energized by...

5. call on others to...

6. make an impact in the following area/field/community etc...

7. face...

8. honour...

9. achieve...

10. make a priority...

11. make a plan for...

12. complete...

13. be deeply touched by the following things/people/events/ideas...

Now looking at what you wrote down for the coming 12 months. In the space below make a note of what will help you create the results you identified in these statements in terms of specific actions.

When you compare your answers in the first half of the exercise (those for the past 12 months) with those for the coming 12 months, what I hope you notice is the following:

to achieve what you set out over the coming months will require your heart and mind working together.

Look back over the previous year's answers where you may have left some blanks. Note where you struggled and why. In my experience where people stall, procrastinate and sabbotage their success correspond to areas where there is conflict between what the heart truly desires and what the mind decides to focus on. When either the heart or the mind tries to move forward without the other, the person suffers. It is likely that looking forward you may have far less blanks or no blanks at all. This is because as you're reading this book, your heart and mind have awaken and are making their respective voices and needs heard. The Grid will help you fuels them both.

WRAP UP

Having done the exercises above, you will now have more clarity about the sort of environment and lifestyle you want to live, who to call on for help, and who you can offer help to. You should also have a clear idea about some of your goals for the year ahead, or what's important for you to realise from the perspective of your heart and mind. You can now take this information and begin to create a satisfying life.

GRIDDING

62

LET'S GET GRIDDING!

Here is what a blank Grid looks like – simple isn't it? A Grid is a page with four areas.

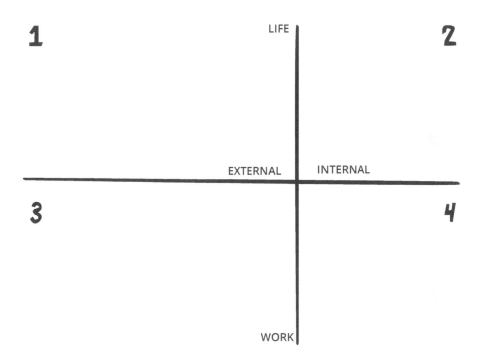

In this workbook, I will show you how to make two types of Grid - a Year Grid and a Month Grid. We will use the Year Grid as a larger blueprint for your life and the Month Grid as a tool to live your balanced life on a daily basis.

First: the Year Grid. This is where you will write down the key things you want to take responsibility for realising over the next 12 months - both in life and at work, for yourself and with others. It is your roadmap to help you work and live in balance.

YEAR GRID

Below is an example of a Year Grid.

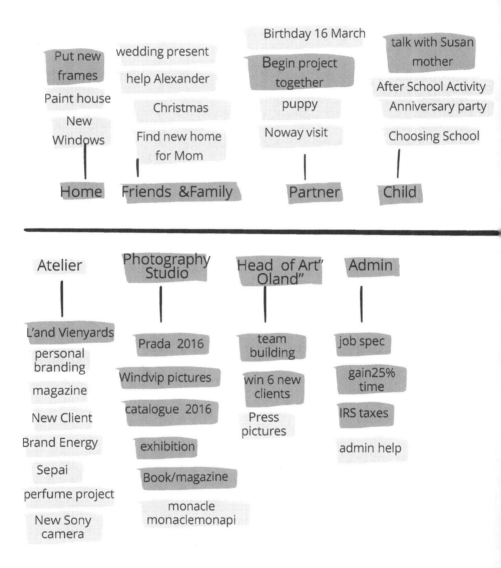

Put new frames
Paint house
New Windows

wedding present
help Alexander
Christmas
Find new home for Mom

Birthday 16 March
Begin project together
puppy
Noway visit

talk with Susan mother
After School Activity
Anniversary party
Choosing School

Home   **Friends &Family**   **Partner**   **Child**

Atelier

Photography Studio

Head of Art' Oland"

Admin

L'and Vienyards
personal branding
magazine
New Client
Brand Energy
Sepai
perfume project
New Sony camera

Prada 2016
Windvip pictures
catalogue 2016
exhibition
Book/magazine
monacle monaclemonapi

team building
win 6 new clients
Press pictures

job spec
gain25% time
IRS taxes
admin help

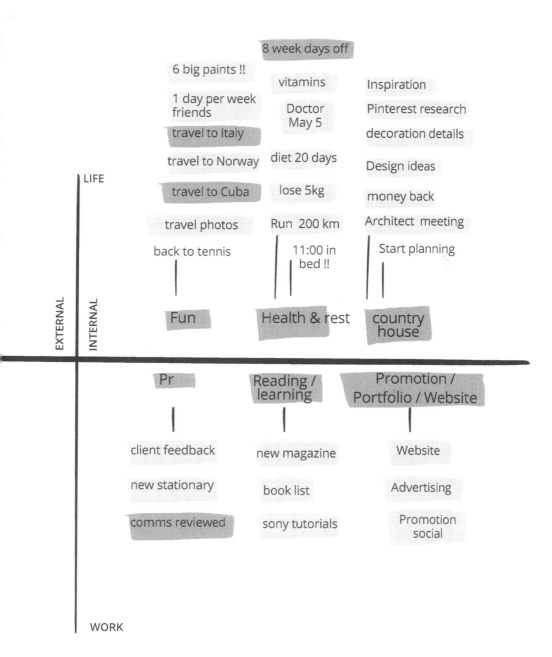

8 week days off

6 big paints !!

vitamins

Inspiration

1 day per week friends

Doctor May 5

Pinterest research

travel to Italy

decoration details

travel to Norway

diet 20 days

Design ideas

travel to Cuba

lose 5kg

money back

travel photos

Run 200 km

Architect meeting

back to tennis

11:00 in bed !!

Start planning

LIFE

EXTERNAL

INTERNAL

Fun

Health & rest

country house

Pr

Reading / learning

Promotion / Portfolio / Website

client feedback

new magazine

Website

new stationary

book list

Advertising

comms reviewed

sony tutorials

Promotion social

WORK

MONTH GRID (OCTOBER)

Below you can see an example of a Month Grid. Notice that the Home Bases stay constant between the Year Grid and the Month Grid and yet the activities for the Month Grid are far more specific. They are now tasks that can be done in one go giving them and the Grid-owner real focus. The Year Grid activities are more general such as 'Norway holiday' or 'new clients' .

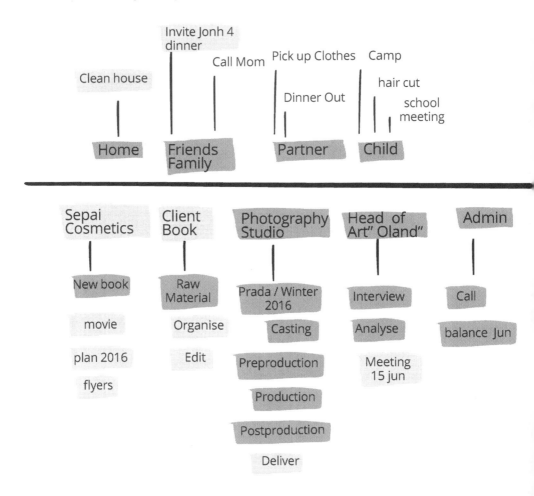

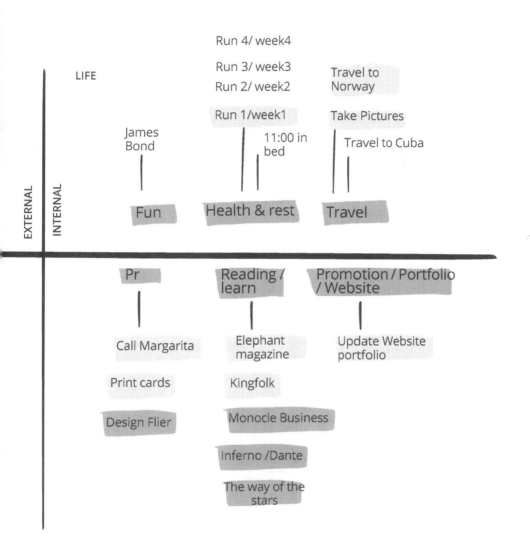

LIFE

Run 4/ week4

Run 3/ week3
Run 2/ week2

Travel to
Norway

Run 1/week1

Take Pictures

James
Bond

11:00 in
bed

Travel to Cuba

EXTERNAL   INTERNAL

Fun

Health & rest

Travel

Pr

Reading /
learn

Promotion / Portfolio
/ Website

Call Margarita

Elephant
magazine

Update Website
portfolio

Print cards

Kingfolk

Design Flier

Monocle Business

Inferno /Dante

The way of the
stars

67

MAKING YOUR OWN YEAR GRID

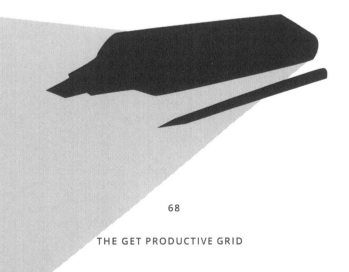

THE GET PRODUCTIVE GRID

YOUR LIFE IS A BLANK PAGE: FILL IT WITH WHAT YOU WANT AND NEED

Now you are ready to draw up your own Year Grid. You'll need a blank piece of paper. I use a sheet of A3 or A4. You can use an empty page in your diary or a notebook or you can use graph paper - the choice is yours. You will also need a pencil, pen and some highlighter pens.

If you are using a tablet, you'll need an app that allows you to write and draw freely rather than one which is purely text-based. Personally, I would advocate a paper-based Grid so that you can have it to hand easily for reference. Accessibility is one of the key factors to making the Grid work for you. But if you travel everywhere with your iPad, that may be your best bet.

The bottom line is this: you are more likely to look at your Grid if it's in a notebook you use on a daily basis such as a paper diary, on your iPad or on your pinboard rather than tucked away on your computer desktop in a text file.

The brain is primarily guided by visual cues.
Nerve cells devoted to visual processing take up about 30%
of the brain real estate compared with just 8% for touch
and 3% for hearing and less than 1% for smell.

Seeing is a powerful form of sensory reasoning. The Grid provides you with instant clarity about your overall agenda, an easy overview of your progress and access to your key priorities - all in one place.

Whatever format you choose, have your Grid to hand like a roadmap to help you navigate your daily life and keep you on track for your goals and dreams. This will become particularly important once we move on to the Month Grid.

DRAWING YOUR GRID LINES TO CREATE FOUR KEY AREAS

THE HORIZONTAL AXIS: DIVIDES 'WORK' AND 'LIFE'.

Take your sheet of paper, turn it on its side to 'landscape' format and draw a horizontal line across it. This is your work-life balance demarcation – 'life' above the line, 'work' below. I put life above work as work has always been designed to support life and not the other way around. As you will soon realise, the Grid will easily tell you whether your life needs more or different work or whether your work supports you having the life you desire or keeps you from it.

The Grid horizontal line also creates a clear delineation in our minds between work and life as two important areas with their own goals and projects. This allows us to give our attention to all the things that matter to us – not just what's in our in-tray.

On your horizontal line write a time of day that marks your transition point from focusing on work to life. On my Grid, the boundary is often at 4pm, but it changes according to the seasons because of natural light and/or my workload and life needs. This line is your reminder to transfer your focus from one domain to the other.

If you are often still at your desk at 10pm then pick a transition time that's a positive but realistic improvement – say 8pm or 6pm.

THE VERTICAL AXIS: DIVIDES EXTERNAL AND INTERNAL GOALS

Now draw a vertical line on your Grid towards the right side of your paper canvas (as shown on the template on page 73). Your Grid will now have four quadrants. This line differentiates the internal things you do to look after your wellbeing (Areas 2 and 4 on the right) from the external projects and activities (Areas 1 and 3 on the left) you carry out for and with others (See the illustration on page 64-67). In other words, items in Areas 2 and 4 are those that refuel you!

Here your energy gets restored. Items in Area 1 and 3 generally spend your energy.

We are often judged on our external results - the new kitchen we've put in or the report we have filed - because they are visible. As a result, we often prioritise the things that fall on the left of the Grid (those that take energy from us) over the things we do to look after ourselves, on the right (activities that help refuel our energy. And yet it takes a healthy, thriving person who is in good health and professional standing (all the Grid activities in Areas 2 and 4) to deliver what is done in Area 1 and 3. Remember that what you put in Area 2 and Area 4 are just as vital as Area 1 and Area 3. And, so is making time to do them.

Note: where exactly you place your horizontal and vertical lines on the page depends on how much space you need in each quadrant for your goals and tasks. Again, don't worry about getting it perfect on the first go. Your perfect Grid will emerge as you experiment–the Gridding process is a form of self-discovery.

71

ALLOCATING SPACES FOR YOUR KEY GOALS WITH HOME BASES

HOME BASES: YOUR 'GOAL KEEPERS'

A Home Base is an umbrella term to house a series of related tasks. 'Exercise' 'holiday', 'family' 'promotion', 'professional skills', 'home', 'Project X', 'health', 'career move', 'wedding', 'travel' make good Home Bases. On your Grid, each Home Base is drawn as a box, as you can see on the Grid examples pictured.

We will shortly be looking at specific tasks within your Home Bases, but for now let's stick with these umbrella headings. Come up with a list of Home Bases that suit you personally and add them to your Grid in the correct quadrant as shown in the example on page 64. The Home Bases listed there are ideas. You may want to use them as inspiration or make up your own. The idea behind a Home Base is that it is something that can't be done in one go but something we work towards that we value. These Home Bases are explained in greater detail below.

THE GET PRODUCTIVE GRID

SAMPLE HOME BASES FOR YOUR GRID

AREA 1.

Family, Friends, Home, Partner,

Parents, Kids, 25th Anniversary, Wedding

AREA 2.

Me-time, Health, Rest, Fun, Creativi-

ty, Fitness, Music, Yoga, Help

AREA 3.

Project X, Business, Admin, Clients,

Key Accounts, Writing, Speaking, Char-

ity work, Volunteering, New Hires.

AREA 4.

Career development, Career expo-

sure, PR, Training, Education, Con-

ferences, Non Executive Positions,

Qualifications, Degree, Awards.

MATCHING HOME BASES WITH SPECIFIC AREAS

AREA 1. EXTERNAL GOALS IN MY PERSONAL LIFE.

These are broad headings that concern your life outside of work.

Examples: Home, Friends, Family, Partner, Holidays, House Move, Dad's 70th, Garden, Loft Conversion

AREA 2. INTERNAL GOALS FOR PERSONAL WELLBEING

Put here all the things you want to do to nurture your body and soul. Many people give energy to work and other people, they run households or community initiatives, work long hours but leave little time or give no attention to self renewal other than eating and sleeping. This Area highlights the importance of looking after yourself so that you are well placed to look after others and to create what you desire in your life. You may notice that some activities are there just for you - and this is the point! They serve to refuel, revitalise, relax and inspire you. Only you know what they are and what you need.

Examples: Me-time, Health, Rest, Fun, Creativity, Fitness, Music, Yoga, Sport,

AREA 3. EXTERNAL GOALS IN MY WORK LIFE

This section contains the things you need to do whether for your employer, your own business, or to make a living. This may also include work that you don't get paid for necessarily but which builds up towards your career or professional work in the future. This Area encourages Gridders to take responsibility and see themselves as active leaders and shapers of their professional output and projects.

Examples: Project X, Business, Admin, Clients, Key Accounts, Writing, Speaking, Charity Work, Volunteering, New Hires.

THE GET PRODUCTIVE GRID

75

AREA 4. INTERNAL GOALS TO SUPPORT PROFESSIONAL WELLBEING

This section refers to the things you need to keep yourself professionally nourished and skilled. These activities support your professional development, ensure you feel confident about your skill set and also help you look after your career (this is something we often forget to do proactively). This box often contains activities and practices that help you be and remain employable or recognised as a pro.

Examples: Career Development, Recognition, Career Exposure, PR, Training, Education, Conferences, Non-Executive Positions, Qualifications, Degrees, Awards.

NOTE: The easiest place to get the hang of Home Bases, is by starting with the bottom right quadrant (Area 4). This section refers to your work and in particular the elements which support your professional wellbeing. I invite my clients to make a 'CPD' – Career Professional Development - box here as a Home Base. But choose whatever headings fit you best.

Complete all four Areas in whichever order you like

Now you have a completed Year Grid with Home Bases in each of the four Areas. Your Home Bases are unique to you and reflect your life. There are no right or wrong answers here. Below, we will learn how to expand your Home Bases into specific activities.

You'll notice that with the Grid method
*we don't talk about **deadlines**.*

When you master the Grid way of working and living,
*deadlines **no longer** run your life – you do!*

NOTE: We're often in a rush to do more on the left-hand side of the Grid. Be aware that when this happens, the right hand Areas suffer which means you will suffer. This can mean feeling tired, run down, resentful, overlooked at work, undervalued, or uncertain about your employability. These are all signs that as the architect of your life you have somehow forgotten to look after yourself. Some people expect others to do this for them but - assuming everyone is an adult - looking after our wellbeing is fundamentally our own responsibility. The Grid helps you do that so you can maintain your performance long-term and look after others as well.

TURNING DREAMS INTO ACTION WITH TASKS

FROM HOME BASES TO SPECIFIC TASKS

Take each Home Base and expand it into key things you want to realise in that field in the coming 12 months. So for example, in Area 1 you may have a Home Base called 'Home'. You could expand this into two specific tasks such as: 'hallway renovation' and 'front garden planting'.

I always have a 'Holidays' Home Base in Area 1 and expand it into a series of tasks covering the important holidays I don't want to forget to plan, such as 'winter break' 'Easter, 'summer', 'autumn retreat' and 'pre-Christmas'. Even if eventually I have more breaks, the Year Grid helps ensure that at least I won't have forgotten to plan the key ones. And when you have a full life, holidays often do take planning.

TIP: There is no right or wrong way to create a Grid, apart from the four key quadrants. You are creating your own system and it will reflect your personality, so experiment and have fun. Eventually you will settle on a style that suits you both in terms of look and content.

THE GET PRODUCTIVE GRID

MAGDALENA BAK - MAIER

COMPLETED YEAR GRID: YOUR LIFE ON ONE PAPER CANVAS

Your completed Year Grid represents everything you want and need to do over the next 12 months. You'll see that the Grid is far more than a to-do list. On this single paper canvas you have captured everything that needs your attention across all the roles you play – whether that's as a parent, partner, friend, mentor, entrepreneur, employee, community member, artist, student and beyond.

You have identified the Home Bases that keep you in top form professionally and personally and the key goals that you want to achieve within them.

Imagine your brain having to stay on top of all this information – and now think of all the energy you have saved yourself in setting it down on your Grid. This is energy that you can now direct more productively – through bringing this glorious canvas to life. The Grid also helps you view your life and consider whether what's on your Grid reflects what you really want. I often use the Grid to help my clients transition from what they *have* towards what they *want*.

FINAL CHECK

Before we declare your Grid ready to go, take a look at it and consider whether it captures everything that needs your attention. In today's hectic life it's way too easy just to focus on the 'have tos' rather than the 'want tos' – even for Gridders! Make sure your Grid has enough 'want tos'.

Remember the Grid covers the things you want in the next 12 months. You may notice that some Home Bases need to be moved off the Grid for now as they simply don't fit in that time frame. Make any adjustments you need. Nothing is ever forgotten in a Grid but everything is given a more realistic time frame.

BRINGING YOUR GRID TO LIFE WITH COLOURFUL HIGHLIGHTING

Now for the fun part. Take a highlighter or several and highlight all your Home Bases. Leave the specific tasks uncoloured for now. The highlighting process is highly significant in Gridding. It is a way of marking your commitment to each Home Base, saying 'I take responsibility for creating the life I want - all systems go!' and later, ticking off your progress through tasks you have completed.

With the Home Bases highlighted, your Grid is now active: a canvas which collects colour and reveals a powerful picture of the activity and progress in your life.

As you complete or realise each task box over time, highlight it. Regular highlighting of completions helps celebrate your achievement and progress. With each item, the highlighter marks another step towards creating a balanced, nurturing and holistically productive life - The life you may not have thought possible and now made real by you.

As time progresses, the Grid fills up with highlighted tasks marking all that has been done and revealing what's left to be tackled. This gives you, the Grid-owner, a wonderful sense of progress and overview of your entire activity in one place. Gridders report a high degree of satisfaction, calm and achievement from using Grids to support their life and work because everything they want to realise, all that matters is always in front of them and it is being *taken care of.*

WORKING YOUR GRID:
HOW DO I KNOW WHICH TASK TO TACKLE FIRST?

Look at your Grid and pick a task you want to do – one you are actually drawn to. Don't overthink it; your immediate goal is just to pick one task, get it done and highlight it (no more feeling overwhelmed, panicked or frustrated at the prospect of what you 'have' to do). Follow the energy and trust that anything you do is good because it is on your Grid.

The Grid improves efficiency because you are automatically drawn to tasks according to your energy levels. Surfing your energy builds motivation and stamina to tackle the tasks you would normally procrastinate over.

Highlighting creates momentum – the more you do, the more you want to do.

Because your Grid contains 'work' and 'life' activities (including things that support and refuel you) your energy is less likely to flag. In fact, you will notice that working your Grid *builds* energy. Most Gridders find they become much more efficient at work and have much more free time because they get more done - faster.

Once you have completed the first task, follow what you are drawn to as a way of selecting what to do next. With this approach, you are tapping into what your heart and mind recognise as important and where they agree. You are also tackling things your body and mind are ready for thus eliminating resistance. This way of working will have a profound effect on your productivity and wellbeing.

The Czech psychologist Mihaly Csikszentmihalyi calls this way of working and being 'flow'.

Let me give you an example from my own life of how I follow my natural energy. Sometimes I don't feel like cracking on with a big project first thing in the morning. But after I have booked a surprise flower delivery for my partner, I feel inner joy for sharing love and my state of mind changes. I look at the Grid and tackling the big work project now through a specific task is not just easier, it is in fact what I *feel* up for. In other words, doing one thing helps me arrive at a state of ease to tackle another without much effort. I feel energised and don't see the project as something to struggle with or force myself to do, but something I really *want to* do and feel ready for. And this is why Gridders break free from deadlines. As they become efficient and work with their energy, they complete things ahead of time using a combination of planning and working with their heart and mind.

Remember earlier [on page 19] we talked about how we tend to resist change? Well, now you don't have to. The Grid puts you in a state of flow, where you quite naturally follow what you feel like doing, while still always working on something important (otherwise it would not be on your Grid!). Resistance falls away; the energy with which you approach each task shifts from a reluctant 'No' to a welcoming 'Yes'. Quite simply, you do a better job more quickly, with more free time at the end of it. The Grid helps every one of its users to be productive and to thrive. It makes people say yes! to things more often because they feel in control and more creative.

'flow'.

85

MAGDALENA BAK - MAIER

ADVANCING BALANCE AND ACTION WITH THE MONTH GRID

TASK

THE MONTH GRID: LET THE REAL MAGIC BEGIN

You've completed your Year Grid; now you have a powerful macro picture of your goals. Next, we're going to make a Month Grid. This will be your biggest ally on a day-to-day basis over the next weeks. Here, your big ideas for your life translate into more immediate and tangible tasks. And this is what separates achievers from dreamers. Those who realise things, simply take action more often. And those who do so consistently are those who take action across all the Grid Areas so that they work and live in balance.

MONTH GRID (OCTOBER)

Below you can see an example of a Month Grid. Notice that the Home Bases stay constant between the Year Grid and the Month Grid and yet the activities for the Month Grid are far more specific. They are now tasks that can be done in one go giving them and the Grid-owner real focus. The Year Grid activities are more general such as 'Norway holiday' or 'new clients' .

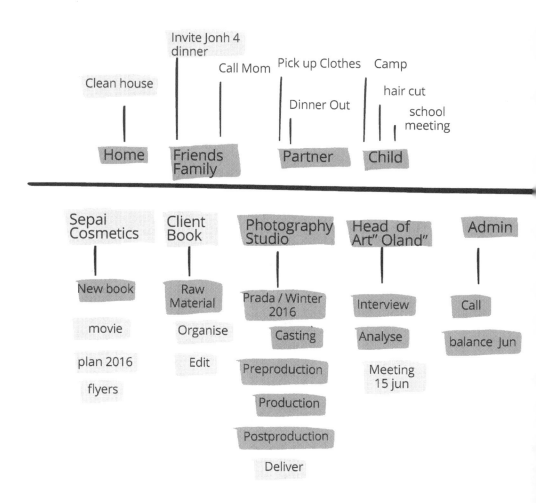

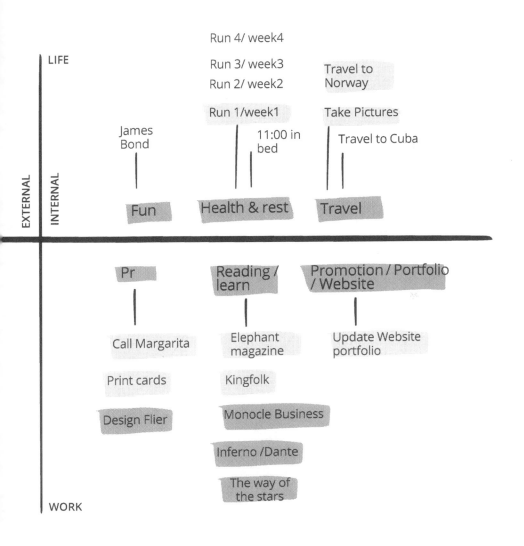

Run 4/ week4

Run 3/ week3

Run 2/ week2

Travel to
Norway

Run 1/week1

Take Pictures

11:00 in
bed

Travel to Cuba

James
Bond

Fun   Health & rest   Travel

LIFE

EXTERNAL   INTERNAL

WORK

Pr   Reading /
learn   Promotion / Portfolio
/ Website

Call Margarita   Elephant
magazine   Update Website
portfolio

Print cards   Kingfolk

Design Flier   Monocle Business

Inferno /Dante

The way of
the stars

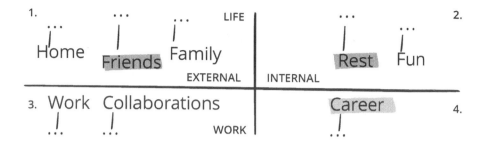

1.

... ... LIFE

Home Friends Family

EXTERNAL | INTERNAL

3. Work Collaborations

... ... WORK

... ...

Rest Fun 2.

Career 4.

...

An example of a completed Month Grid is on page 66 and as rough sketch to help you start is above. Take a new blank page and as with the Year Grid, start with lines and your key Home Bases but this time in relation to the coming four weeks or calendar month. You may also want to give your Month Grid a title such as 'April Grid'.

QUICK RECAP OF WHAT TO DO TO MAKE YOUR MONTH GRID

1. Put your Home Bases in each quadrant. They will be the same as those on your Year Grid*.
2. Expand each Home Base by writing down tasks related to it that can be done in the timeframe of the Month Grid **.
3. Mark your commitment to the Grid by highlighting your Home Bases.
4. Now study your Month Grid, and choose a task box, which attracts you.
5. Place the Grid somewhere obvious and visually accessible – on your pinboard, in your handbag, above your work area, on your desk – so you can use it daily to support your progress.

For example, if you are a writer, then your Year Grid and your Month Grid may have a Home Base called 'Writing'.

** *Ensure each task box corresponds to a single task that can be done in 'one go'. This is very important in the Month Grid. Where the Year Grid boxes may be mega tasks, the Month Grid boxes are small enough to complete in one go. In addition, you may wish to subdivide further. So for example, if you have a box for Yoga you may want to partition the yoga box into segments so that you can highlight one of them after every Yoga session. One of the key demotivators is working hard and not seeing progress. The task way of Gridding helps you avoid this trap.*

You're ready to go!

Here are a few examples of how the Year and Month Grids have changed people's thinking and brought them greater balance.

"*I know that over the next month my work will be highly demanding, so I automatically focus on tasks that will help me pace my energy and refuel [activities in Area 2 - personal wellbeing]. I may schedule more short but effective tasks such as a mindful walk home in the fresh air, or a tea in the garden or a glass of wine looking through my favourite magazine so that I can refuel for the next activity. While in the past I might have neglected my significant others during busy times, thinking I will make it up to them, the Grid makes sure they stay a top priority even when I have little time. Not only does this recharge me, but it ensures that I am not neglecting the things that I have identified as significant in my life - such as friends and family or my health.*"

"*My work schedule over the coming weeks looks manic. This means that the home task I really want to do either is best postponed for another month, or needs to be delegated. Now I can see this and make appropriate plans. Instead of work forcing me to postpone the task, I can hire a painter and use the time to finish a project for work. We [my family] will have a new hallway and I will feel on top of my work assignment.*"

THE GET PRODUCTIVE GRID

"My partner's 50th is coming up and there is a massive amount of planning. It's a job in itself and I feel tired. What I need is help to pull it off and also some time for me to help me recharge. I will book a massage and give myself a quiet evening of TLC. Also a couple of early nights will help. I have made early nights into a box and gave it four divisions. Will make sure to ask the kids to help with breakfast the next mornings."

"The holiday to Australia will cost us £7000. To make this happen we need to save on a regular basis. My monthly Grid will make this a priority. Thursday night dates out will now be special dinners with candlelight at home and the money put away for the holiday."

94

FIVE KEY GRIDDING TIPS

Here are five tips to ensure your Grids support you

1. REMEMBER: A TASK IS SOMETHING YOU CAN DO IN ONE SITTING (WHETHER THAT'S MINUTES OR HOURS)

Check that this is true for all your Month Grid tasks. If this is not the case, you need to break the task down further.

NOTE: It can take a couple of goes to get the hang of this, so be patient with yourself. You may want to divide some tasks into a series of boxes (like bricks in a wall) so that your work always merits a highlighted finish. For example, if you want to go to the gym three times a week, you could sudivide the 'gym' box into 12 segments on your Month Grid (one for each visit). Then you can highlight a brick every time you hit the gym. If the number is not too high you can also make a box for each go as in the example on pg xxx Month Grid with 4 runs.

Clue: If you spend a lot of time working but can't highlight any specific box as complete, it's a sign that your tasks are not true tasks. Highlighting is the fun and rewarding part, which keeps your motivation going.

2. ALWAYS 'TIMEFRAME' YOUR GRID

We have looked at a Year Grid and Month Grid, but you might find that a different time frame works better for you e.g. a fortnightly Grid or a three-month Grid. Whatever the time span, mark this at the top of your Grid. Keeping to your time frame helps set goals that fit to the time you have, maintains focus and helps you progress more effectively. Giving your Grid a specific time frame also helps you to stay realistic, which is vital. People lose momentum and get discouraged because they underestimate what they can do in the long term and hugely overestimate what they can achieve in the short term. The Grid will help you see that and correct it over time as you get to know how you work towards what you want.

3. RESIST TEMPTATION TO ADD TO YOUR GRID

One of the reasons people love the Grid is that it makes them more efficient. This generates free time for creativity or even additional work. Having a Grid makes it easier to say YES to new activities in a way that won't overwhelm or add to a massive pile of things to do.

As a rule of thumb it's OK to add to the Grid so long as you can honestly say that doing so won't compromise your overall balance. If you get that sinking feeling that your Grid is empty of colour and you're adding more, then stop and reconsider.

Remember, the point of the horizontal line separating 'work' and 'life' in the Grid is to support quality time for yourself, including rest. If adding more tasks to your work areas (Areas 3 and 4) begins to shift the horizontal line upwards, it means that your work is overshooting the boundary you have given it. Similarly, if your life is beginning to affect your work then it's a sign to pay attention as imbalance has crept in.

If you really want to add something to the Grid in any of the Areas, consider the impact of it across the entire Grid.

NOTE: often we make unhealthy compromises and neglect our own wellbeing or our home life in favour of work. If you are squeezing more and more tasks into Areas 1 and 3, your Grid will flag that up. The highlighting provides a powerful visual warning that your balance is at risk. While some people may suffer from overbooking Areas 2 and 4, this is rare in my experience. Either way, aim for balance across all four Areas that reflects the life you want to live and one where your ability to restore energy is not compromised.

MAGDALENA BAK - MAIER

4. WORK THE FOUR QUADRANTS SIMULTANEOUSLY

Are you highlighting in all sectors equally? Does each quadrant have at least some colour?

The Grid helps reveal balance or lack of it in your life.

Perhaps there are some tasks with no color which you are ignoring? If so ask yourself Why? Often, when we are out of balance, it can be hard to think of activity for certain areas. For example, people who work too much begin to struggle to identify things that are "fun" or "play" or justify rest. And yet each of these activities is vital for one's wellbeing. If you find yourself in a situation where some of your four Grid Areas have very few tasks because you can't think of any, be patient with yourself. Ask others for ideas. Don't be afraid to experiment. If you are resisting certain tasks, ask yourself how come? The visual cues the highlighting provides protect you from losing balance. For holistic productivity, we need to attend to all aspects of our lives - which means the four quadrants.

5. CREATE YOUR NEXT GRID SO YOU ARE NEVER WITHOUT ONE

People often start well in their first Grid month and love the results they are generating. But early results often disappear as they think they can now work the next month without one. Without another Grid to support them, they quickly fall back into ineffectiveness, working on things that matter far less than they realise, procrastinating on tasks and losing balance. Their thriving life begins to suffer. It takes at least three to four Month Grids for gridding to become a habit.

You'll find that each Grid takes progressively less time to create. Often your second or third Grid takes only a few minutes, saving you hours of time in the long run.

Make a diary entry to remind yourself to draw up your next Grid, or put it in as a task box on your current Grid.

THREE MOST FREQUENT QUESTIONS PEOPLE NEW TO GRIDDING ASK

1. CAN YOU HELP ME UNDERSTAND THE DIFFERENCE BETWEEN AREAS 3 AND 4 WHEN IT COMES TO WORK?

The distinction that I make when it comes to the vertical line of the Grid is in relation to energy. To the right are activities and tasks that refuel energy and to the left of the vertical line are those that expand it. A simple rule of thumb when it comes to work and where to put things in relation to these two areas of the Grid can be to place activities you get paid for in Area 3. Activities related to work that you do in service of your mastery - often where you are not paid or have to fund them yourself – in Area 4. For example, your work projects and things you are having to deliver as part of your role, employment, contracts, creative portfolio etc will end up on the left in Area 3, while you taking an evening class to master Adobe Illustrator or how to write a novel will end up in Area 4. What is interesting when looking at people who remain fresh at work is that they regularly top up their energy through learning and development (Area 4 activities). It's where they draw inspiration, ideas and energy as well as make fruitful links with people and new opportunities. Those who fail to attend to such activities, tire, grow stale and eventually lose their vibrancy and edge.

THE GET PRODUCTIVE GRID

2. WHERE DO I PUT HOLIDAYS, IN AREA 1 OR 2?

As in the example above, this question concerns the ability to grasp the concept of energy refueling versus energy expanding activities; in other words what's to the left and right of the top section of the Grid. When it comes to Holidays, what's far more important is that they end up on the Grid in the first place as opposed to where you put them. But here's an elaboration on the distinction to help clarify this further. Imagine the energy and effort that goes into organizing each holiday. If you are someone who can brief your assistant or travel agent to arrange everything for you so that all you are left to do is pack and enjoy it, then I would suggest that you park your Holidays in Area 2. But if holidays for you include sitting up a few evenings researching destinations on Trip Advisor, e-mailing property owners to land your perfect home away from home and coordinating the bookings for your entire family plus two friends then I would suggest you put holidays in Area 1.

3. I'M A TAD CONFUSED ON WHEN TO USE THE HIGHLIGHTER?

Ok. When you draw up a new Grid, you highlight all the Home Bases and that's it. This act brings your Grid into life. After this however, the Highlighter only comes into play when you actually tackle and finish a task on your Grid. You will of course find yourself on numerous occasions doing things that are not on your Grid and so when you complete them, there will be nothing to highlight. If these tasks are part of your normal routine and they benefit you, perhaps they do not need Gridding in the first place. For example, I don't exactly Grid my morning routine and yet I manage to complete it day in and day out. The point of the Grid is not to include every tiny task you do. That would be exhaustive and unhelpful. The Grid comes into its own when it is filled with your purposeful agenda that reminds you of what you need and want to get done that can easily turn to driftwood against the daily realities of your life. So each time you highlight what is on your Grid you acknowledge the master and hero within you that succeeded in attending to what you know and value.

3 M O N T H S
R E V I E W

THE GET PRODUCTIVE GRID

HOW TO KNOW YOUR GRID IS HELPING YOU

This section of the workbook is for you to work through after you have completed three consecutive Month Grids.

Here, we will take stock of the progress you made and look at what this reveals about you to help you pinpoint where you might want to improve. At the end of this section are my parting creative exercises to help you get to know your heart and mind further. The more you know about yourself, the better your Grids can work to support you.

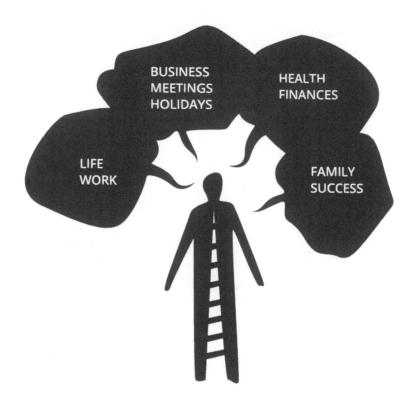

TAKING STOCK

It's extremely satisfying to be able to look over past Grids as they give you a clear picture about the important things coming up for you in your life. You never lose sight of your priorities because they are staring you in the face (you only have to look at your Home Bases!). When we're under pressure, it's easy to get our priorities confused or to work on something that is not, in fact, high priority at all. With the Grid, you always have an aide memoir of what's important - and this will help you present yourself effectively and stay balanced, especially when the going gets tough.

When you look back over the past three Month Grids, you might notice the Home Bases that never change. Equally you may find that one or two Home Bases fall away entirely as completed projects. In their place you may now have a new Home Base. This is one of the beautiful aspects of the Grid method. Using Grids helps you notice how your activities and the energy you give moves you forward, giving you cause to celebrate. At times they also help reveal just how much work and energy things require to progress. And that's important also. Many people underestimate how long things will take and risk feeling drained by it.

Many of the constant Home Bases - such as 'friends' and 'home' - will change in terms of the activities or tasks within them. As you review the three months you will see the many ways in which you have advanced these vital areas in spite of having a full agenda.

I encourage my clients to sit down and reflect on the Grids they have recently completed and see the picture they reveal.

105

Here are some of the things that typically come up during a review. I encourage you to have a think about them also.

NATURAL ENERGISERS
• Activities you enjoy and always tackle first, which again begins to reveal what naturally energises you and what you gravitate towards.

GAPS
• Areas that you naturally neglect or that remain unhighlighted even after three months. These pinpoint a deeper resistance, which may require further support.

SUPERHERO SYNDROME
• Home Bases where you've been overly ambitious and assigned yourself too many tasks. This will help you pace yourself in the future. It will also help you recognise the large amount of work required that you may have underestimated. Sometimes, the Grids help pinpoint work that makes the largest difference so you can focus more on that in the future. For example, going to bed by 11pm makes you notice you are more effective and get more done.

PROCRASTINATION
• Activities you typically leave until last, which may reveal how you truly feel about them. This will help you pinpoint things you may have to do or feel you have to do but which you may want to work towards eliminating as the year progresses.

IMBALANCE
• Imbalance across the four quadrants, which highlights where you may need to focus more.

LINK BETWEEN YOUR PRESENT AND YOUR FUTURE
• Take a look at the Year Grid to see how your monthly Grids moved you forward in your larger agenda: be it losing weight, finding balance, changing career or creating a richer social life.

The Grid is a mindful practice of being present to life, work and yourself.
It lays bare the facts of how you shape your life activities and where you need assistance.

"A man who works with
his hands is a laborer;
a man who works
with his hands
and his brain
is a craftsman;
but a man
who works
with his hands
and his brain and
his heart is an artist."

- Louis Nizer -

WHO AM I REALLY?

The Grid helps to reveal who you are and also provides a useful tool to guide your personal development so that the person you want to be is allowed to live fully. The following three exercises are included in this workbook to help you coach yourself towards greater integrity and a life you want using the Grid. I use them in my one-to-one practice and group workshops. Do them when you have three months of Grids behind you. They will help you tap deep wisdom (Activity 1), make your life even better (Activity 2) and shift from *being* good to *doing* good (Activity 3). The same way that the opening exercises helped lay the foundations for the Grid work, these final three activities will help you review and tweak what you have so that you truly create a life that reflects your true spirit, aspiration and potential. You can complete them together or as stand-alone activities.

MAGDALENA BAK - MAIER

ACTIVITY 1: GRID-ASSITED SELF ANALYSIS

Collect your completed monthly Grids and have a look at them. In this task you are going to write an analysis of yourself based on your work in the Grids. When you have completed this, you can check whether what you find feels massively satisfying, less than what you expected or in line with what you want.

Steps to complete in this exercise :

Step 1. Quick analytic sketch

Write a paragraph describing what you see on the Grids as a whole and for each individually. Keep your description fact based and avoid justifying anything. This is easy to do as the Grids are yours. You may find it easy to simply report on activities in each of the four key Grid areas in terms of what's there and also in terms of what is highlighted and what is not highlighted.

Example:

"Mary has everything in Area 1 highlighted and clearly family and friends and her boyfriend matter to her. Her Area 4 also looks impressive though the Master's programme she is on is not highlighted. I can see that Mary enjoyed dancing as this activity shows up in each Monthly Grid and is always highlighted. There are a few items in Area 2 that repeatedly look blank and they are exercise she marked as running and yoga. Mary appears to be juggling a job and her own business. The job has everything completed on all Grids but her business projects contain very little highlighted tasks."

Step 2. Overall Analysis

In the space below write down a one-line headline that would best describe the completed Month Grids. A few examples of how this can be done are given below.

Example:

"Super busy Grid each month and full of color but on the whole pretty balanced across the 4 Areas."

"Balanced Grids with a third of tasks in Box 3 left to highlight each month."

"Box 3 clearly dominates. Where is the Life?"

"Not much in Area 4 in the last three months."

Step 3. Overarching feeling

In the space below write down one word that describes how the three completed Grids make you feel. For example you may feel Proud, Accomplished, Confused, Hopeful, Deflated, Tired etc.

Step 4. Inner Wisdom Counsel

Now connect with the deep wisdom within you. This is not your head talking or your heart but the two aligned together. What advice, question, and guidance does this intelligence offers at this point? Listen in stillness to what bubbles up to the surface and note it down below.

Example:

Advice: "Don't forget to live in the moment."

Question: What do you want to be different for you in six months?

Wisdom: "Rest is an activity."

Inquiry: "Where are you truly showing up at the moment and what does this tell you?"

Guidance: "Go to bed early more often."

Step 5. Action

Having completed the four steps above, what do you want to maintain and/or change in your future Grids to help you thrive even more? Make sure that whatever you come up with becomes incorporated in your next Grid.

THE GET PRODUCTIVE GRID

ACTIVITY 2: LIVING A THRIVING LIFE

Look at your completed Grids and complete the following exercise.
Take a piece of paper and draw a vertical line down the middle so that you have two columns. In the left hand column write down everything you like about what the Grid has shown and how it has happened so that you can now begin to live *on purpose!*

Example:

What I like?

- *I devote time to writing*
- *I made time for my partner and friends*
- *I've taken concrete steps to improve my home*
- *I've completed three projects*

Now, write down what could be even better in your life...

- *My home would be fully finished, white, sleek and modern*
- *I would have a regular column where my articles would be read by others*
- *I would not need to Grid exercise to remind me that it's vital for my wellbeing*
- *I would have enough money to hire help for my creative project*

Again, when you're done, look at the list above and consider what changes, Home Bases or tasks you want to put into your future Grid to help you move closer towards the life you want to live.

ACTIVITY 3: SHIFTING FROM BEING PRODUCTIVE TO LIVING

The problem with some goals is that they can be hugely consuming and absorb the person to a degree where they forget to live in balance with their larger context and their full spirit. This is true even in a well-balanced Grid that is focused on the 'I' or 'me'. As people Grid tasks they may do so with great enthusiasm and vigour and the results fuel their drive further. In doing that, their Grids may fail to take into account that other people in their lives have or may wish to have their own Grids which support their aspirations and needs. Hence what is critical in a well-balanced life is arriving at personal goals and balanced Grids in a way that creates an experience of a good life for the Grid-creator and others around them.

Look at the completed Grids and examine the impact your actions have had on your key relationships. You may want to consider your friends, family, partner, colleagues, neighbours as well as your various communities.

For each person that matters to you, note down the true impact you have had in his or her life over the time period of each Grid you examine.

Example:

Partner - made them feel loved but also made them feel bad for doing less for me.
Colleagues – made them feel insignificant by failing to acknowledge the positive ways in which they have enriched me before I moved to a new role.
Neighbours – made them feel invisible by failing to stop by for a quick hello.
Sister – made her feel loved and cherished by taking time off to be with her when she felt emotionally low, and by listening to her with compassion and love.

Once you have considered the impact you have had on people, you may want to add new actions to your Grid over the coming weeks or months. You may wish to focus on one specific practice such as giving more frequent acknowledgement or refraining from judging others.

Everyone is a genius. But if you judge a fish by its ability to climb a tree, It will spend its whole life believing that it is stupid
- Albert Einstein -

SUMMARY

Our brains consume a great deal of energy. To conserve power, their often run on autopilot unless we focus. This means that to live more *on purpose* we must practice being *conscious* and *mindful.* How satisfied we feel with our life and our work depends directly on how well we apply our mind to the actions we take and how much we attend to what fuels our heart.

Unless we schedule and plan, our actions can become time *fillers* instead of time *makers.* Precious time slips through our fingers and the joys of life pass us by. Plans give us much needed order and free up time. But we *can* have it all - by applying a little structure, by honouring our true aspirations and by taking regular, conscious steps towards realising them. When we combine heart and mind, we make time count!

The Grid is a tool and method to help aid you in this process.

THE GET PRODUCTIVE GRID

*"Wherever you go,
go with all your heart."*

- Confucius -

CONGRATULATIONS, YOU HAVE EARNED YOUR GRID LICENCE!

By working through this book you have completed three months of Grids and have a Year Grid to bring you results, balance and deepen your experience of life. You have learned a great deal about yourself in the process, about what helps you thrive and how you might be keeping yourself from thriving.

I hope that what you have discovered has turned you into a regular Gridder!

Along the way, I hope you have been able to glimse your best self - the self that brings energy and joy into your world and feels your heart open to life and other people in it.

Gridding like all techniques and tools suits some people more than others. It is not for everyone and if you have found that to be true for you, then I am sure the process has still left you clearer in terms of your goals and ways of working that suit your personality and style.

If you liked what the Grid has done for you and how it helps you look after yourself and your life, then keep Gridding!

Now that you know the basics, I give you creative licence to apply the principle in a way that suits you even better. This may take the form of daily mini Grids to help make each day truly balanced, longer time scale Grids (3, 5 or 10 years) for yourself, your family, or your team at work. You may even wish to apply the Grid method to an entire organisation. I would love to hear about your experience. Please contact me at mbm@ maketimecount.com with the subject line: The Get Productive Grid, or connect with me on LinkedIn or Facebook.

I love to hear the many ways in which the Grid is helping to empower people to live a richer life.

119

MAGDALENA BAK - MAIER

WHATEVER YOU DO, NEVER STOP THE WORK, WHICH IS TO KEEP LEARNING ABOUT YOURSELF AND FOLLOWING YOUR HEART. THIS IS YOUR WORK. ONE OF THE MOST REWARDING ASPECTS OF LIFE IS DISCOVERING WHO ONE IS, WHO ONE CAN BECOME AND WHAT ONE CAN MAKE HAPPEN.

BE CURIOUS, BELIEVE, QUESTION, EXPLORE. ALL YOU NEED IS ALREADY WITHIN YOU AND WHEREVER YOU GO, GO WITH ALL YOUR HEART. THE GRID WILL HELP YOU ALONG THE WAY AND WILL BE YOUR LASTING EVIDENCE OF THE YOUR PROGRESS AND THE BALANCED LIFE YOU ARE CREATING – AND LIVING. I WISH YOU HEALTH, SWEET CONTENTMENT AND PROSPERITY.

MAGDALENA

BECOMING
A MASTER
OF PRACTICE

MAGDALENA BAK - MAIER

THE GET PRODUCTIVE GRID

FIVE HOLISTIC PRODUCTIVITY TIPS FROM MY OWN GRID PRACTICE

1. Practice daily affirmations. An affirmation is usually a phrase that declares a specific truth or wisdom. To me they can serve as daily reminders of inspirations and wisdom we need to hold in our minds and hearts to help us lead more resourceful and healthier lives. I highly recommend Louise Hay's 'Daily Thoughts' calendar and/or App. Live these and share them with others. Do a daily Grid to keep yourself in balance.

2. Always start the day with a task that is most important to your wellbeing (Area 2 task), even if you can only devote 15 minutes to it. Begin the task with a powerful affirmation such as "I create best when I am well" and get cracking! And don't forget to share genuine appreciation, generosity and affection with as many people as possible. If you are short on time, practice stillness for a minute to help you centre and to remind you that you are a part of something larger than you.

3. When faced with a big job, identify the first actual step and tackle that! This is enough to not only get you started but ensures you kick into gear and overcome resistance and procrastination. Don't think about the rest of the Task boxes. If you still don't know where to begin, lay out in front of you all the things connected with the task on PostIt notes or as a list, and see what first step emerges. I love markers, color, stickers and stationary aids that help me have fun and stay creative while I tackle projects.

4. Set a clear boundary to mark the end of your work. That Horizontal Grid line really matters, especially in your Month Grid. Be clear about at least one Life item that you are looking forward to enjoying at the end of each day. You may still overshoot the actual time, but having a boundary will help you become more efficient. And honor your commitments especially those you make to children and loved ones. Remember most work is not that important unless you are saving a life that very minute.

5. Remember, there will be many people who have trodden a similar road to yours and those who came before you. They have faced similar tasks and have found effective strategies for to cope and succeed. They carry wisdom of experience you can only gain by getting older. Save some time and take them out for tea. Often they are only too happy to share their knowledge. Accept help if you are struggling - and in turn extend help to others as much as you can. Always practice genuine connection. It's where life dwells.

FIND MAGDALENA BAK-MAIER AT

Twitter: maketimecountuk

Facebook: www.facebook.com/maketimecountltd

Youtube: www.youtube.com/c/Maketimecount

Programmes: www.maketimecount.com

1:1 coaching: www.maketimecount.com

Blog: www.maketimecount.com

OTHER BOOKS BY MAGDALENA

Get Productive! How to get things done and boost your productivity,
Capstone 2013 www.amazon.co.uk

RECOMMENDED BOOKS BY OTHER AUTHORS

Start with Why: How Great Leaders Inspire Everyone to Take Action by Simon Sinek

Do the Work by Steven Pressfield

Your Brain at Work by David Rock

Love by Leo Buscaglia

How to be a Happy Human by Dr. Pam Spurr

WAYS TO CONTINUE YOUR GRID PRACTICE

• Read this book and experiment with Grids yourself. Invite a friend or colleague to do it with you and compare your results and insights at regular intervals.

• Join one of my teleconference groups and connect with people from around the world as you use the Grid to make your life more balanced, healthy and holistically productive.

• Join an on-line course.

• Consider training as a Certified Make Time Count Grid Facilitator.

• Attend an in-person workshop with Me, the Grid inventor.

• Get in touch for ways in which you can help us take the Grid into the world to serve humanity.

You can find more info about all of these at www.maketimecount.com or get in touch by E-mail: info@maketimecount.com

ABOUT MAKE TIME COUNT

Magdalena founded Make Time Count Ltd in 2013 dedicated to the idea that best performance, success and wellbeing emerge when heart and mind work together. Make Time Count is a philosophy, growing organisation and an ecosystem. Its mission is to help individuals and organisations create conditions and have tools to thrive and develop their talent. The space gathers like-minded individuals, practitioners, organisations and those who share our values: results, genuine connection, integrity, craftsmanship and learning.

HELP ME SPREAD HEART AND MIND WORK

My work is dedicated to helping people and organisations connect heart and mind and live it. This can be done through speaker engagements, consultancy, in-house and long-distance training, Train-the-Trainer events and certification programmes that grow our community of Make Time Count teachers and coaches. If you are interested in partnering, collaboration or if you have a social cause where heart and mind work and tools can add value please get in touch with me via mbm@make-timecount.com

Our best way of making a difference is by working together.

130

*"We are what we
do, excellence
then is not an act,
but a habit."*

- Aristotle -

MAGDALENA BAK·MAIER
MAKE TIME COUNT

ACKNOWLEDGEMENTS

I would like to thank the following people for their support, kindness, inspiration and help with this project. First a big thank you goes to Jill Hough who is a treasured gift in my life as a dear friend, gifted counselor, and an angel and to Stefan Maier and Philip Shaw who reminds me on regular basis that angels walk the earth. I'd like to thank Carlos Vieria who is a gifted designer and wonderful friend. With his talents and generous heart, Carlos has added magic to my work with wonderful illustrations that I'm sure my readers will love just as much as I do. I'd also like to thank Victoria Woodhall who after attending my Grid workshop at the start of 2015 connected with me and offered her editorial skills for the project and Sarah Adams - my personal assistant - who believed in my work and sought me out to get involved. In the same spirit, I would also like to thank Kyle Newman, a fellow coach and colleague and friend who is an IT angel behind the scenes. A big thank you also goes to Suzy Grieves, current editor of Psychologies Magazine for believing in the power of my work and helping me share the Grid with more people through an exciting Psychologies Life Labs collaboration. I would like to give a special thanks to my wonderful coach Antony Parry who with his compassionate heart and beautiful soul helps me nurture and uphold my own. Your unshakable belief in my work and what I stand for has been a major gift. I wish to thank the following people for the gift of true friendship: Anna Korre, Brad Cramer, Antonio Kehtar, Iasonas Triantis, Corinna Linzas, Tracey Ward, Kevin Gothelf and Alexandra Almaral – you truly enrich my life and many others. You are part of my growing family. And I'd like to thank my parents for their unconditional love.

I am deeply thankful to many leaders from Imperial College London especially Stephen Richardson, Peter Cawley, Antony Bull and Peter Childs as well as many Alumni of my Academic Development Centre for supporting and encouraging me to take my ideas and work into the world. Deserving a very special mention are Joao Paulo Crespo and Antonio Rendas from NOVA Portugal for believing in my heart and mind approach and to Rita Falcao for logistical support. It has been a pleasure to work with you and see the heart and mind leadership experiment work. I would like to thank countless clients who inspire me with their dreams and who trust me with their hearts. Our collaborations give me great satisfaction. And last but not least, I'd like to thank Marilyn Clarke and Mia Clarke for their love and support.

Finally, a heartfelt thank you goes to you my reader. If this book has ended up in your hands, we are off to an exciting adventure together to help you make time count. The ideas you hold are powerful provided you put them to use. Please always remember that you are never alone. When we dare to create in service of a better world for others as much as ourselves, like-minded souls come to our aid. Look out for them and cherish their presence. Life is nothing more than time spent doing what we love with people we love and those who love us for who we are. Let that circle grow ever wider as you live your Grid.

IF THIS BOOK HAS INSPIRED
OR HELPED YOU, PLEASE PASS IT ON
OR MENTION IT TO SOMEONE
YOU BELIEVE MAY NEED IT.